What Jesus Said and How to Live It

by Mary Faderan

Copyright @2018 Mary Faderan
ISBN:
ISBN-13:
9780692117422

Table of Contents

Chapter	Page
The next day, after Jesus had decided to leave for Galilee, he met Philip and said, "Follow Me". Jn 1:43	1
"Jesus answered, 'Destroy this Temple, and in three days I will raise it up." Jn 2:19	7
"Simon Peter answered, 'Lord, to whom shall we go? You have the message of eternal life, and we believe; we have come to know that you are the Holy One of God.' Jn 6:68-69	17
"Do not be judging according to appearances; let your judgement be according to what is right." Jn 7:24	22
"If you ask me anything in my name, I will do it. If you love me, you will keep my commandments." Jn 14:14-15	27

"I am the true vine, and my Father is the vinedresser. Every branch in me that bears no fruit he cuts away, and every branch that does bear fruit he prunes to make it bear even more."
Jn 15:1-2
                                                                        31

"If the world hates you, you must realize that it hated me before it hated you. If you belonged to the world, the world would love you as its own; but because you do not belong to the world, because my choice of you has drawn you out of the world, that is why the world hates you."
Jn 15:18-19
                                                                        35

"I have told you all this so that you may find peace in me. In the world you will have hardship but be courageous. I have conquered the world."
Jn 16:33
                                                                        40

"Jesus replied, 'You would have no power over me at all if it had not been given you from above.'"
Jn 19:11
                                                                        42

"And Jesus said to them: 'Come after me and I will make you fishers of people.'"
Mk 1:17
                                                                        46

"And he replied, 'Who are my mother and my brothers?' And looking at those sitting in a circle around him, he said, 'Here are my mother and my brothers. Anyone who does the will of God, that person is my brother and sister and mother.'"
Mk 3:33-35

52

"And some seeds fell on rich soil, grew tall, and strong, and produced a good crop; the yield was thirty, sixty, even a hundredfold.' And he said, 'Anyone who has ears for listening should listen.'"
Mk 4:8-9

57

"And if any place does not welcome you and people refuse to listen to you, as you walk away shake off the dust under our feet as evidence to them."
Mk 6:11

63

"What gain, then, is it for anyone to win the whole world and forfeit his life?"
Mk 8:36

68

"For if anyone in this sinful and adulterous generation is ashamed of me and of my words, the Son of man will also be ashamed of him when he comes in the glory of his Father with the holy angels."
Mk 8:37

72

"But anyone who is the downfall of one of these little ones who have faith, would be better thrown into the sea with a great millstone hung round his neck."
Mk 9:42

77

"'My children.' [Jesus] said to them, 'how hard it is to enter the kingdom of God! It is easier for a camel to pass through the eye of a needle than for someone rich to enter the kingdom of God.' They were more astonished than ever, saying to one another, 'In that case, who can be saved?' Jesus gazed at them and said, 'By human resources it is impossible, but not for God, because for God everything is possible.'"
Mk 10:24-27

81

"In his teaching he said, 'Beware of the scribes who like to walk about in long robes, to be greeted respectfully in the market squares, to take the front seats in the synagogues and the places of honour at banquets; these are the men who devour the property of widows and for show offer long prayers. The more severe will be the sentence they receive.'"
Mk 12:38-40

86

"A poor widow came and put in two small coins,   89
the equivalent of a penny. Then he called his
disciples and said to them, 'In truth I tell you; this
poor widow has put more in than all who have
contributed to the treasury; for they have all put in
money they could spare, but she in her poverty
has put in everything she possessed, all she had to
live on."
Mk 12:42-44

"Blessed are you when people abuse you and   92
persecute you and speak all kinds of calumny
against you falsely on my account. Rejoice and be
glad, for your reward will be great in heaven; this
is how they persecuted the prophets before you."
Mt 5:11-12

"You are salt for the earth. But if salt loses its   99
taste, what can make it salty again? It is good for
nothing and can only be thrown out to be
trampled under people's feet."
Mt 5:13

"Therefore, anyone who infringes even one of the   102
least of these commandments and teaches others
to do the same will be considered the least in the
kingdom of Heaven; but the person who keeps
them and teaches them will be considered great in
the kingdom of Heaven."
Mt 5:19

"But I say this to you, if a man looks at a woman lustfully, he has already committed adultery with her in his heart. If your right eye should be your downfall, tear it out and throw it away; for it will do you less harm to lose one part of yourself than to have your whole body thrown into hell."
Mt 5: 29-30   105

"Do not store up treasure for yourselves on earth, where moth and woodworm destroy them and thieves can break in and steal. But store up treasures for yourselves in heaven, where neither moth nor woodworm destroys them and thieves cannot break in and steal. For wherever your treasure is, there will your heart be too."
Mt 6:16   109

"Jesus said to him, 'I will come myself and cure him.' The centurion replied, 'Sir, I am not worthy to have you under my roof; just give the word and my servant will be cured.'"
Mt 8:7-8   115

"And when Jesus reached the house the blind men came up to him and he said to them, 'Do you believe I can do this?' They said, 'Lord, we do.' Then he touched their eyes saying, 'According to your faith, let it be done to you.' And their sight returned."
Mt 9:28-29   120

"So if anyone declares himself for me in the presence of human beings, I will declare myself for him in the presence of my Father in heaven. But the one who disowns me in the presence of human beings, I will disown in the presence of my Father in heaven."
Mt 10:32

123

"Do not suppose that I have come to bring peace to the earth: it is not peace I have come to bring, but a sword. For I have come to set son against mother, daughter-in-law against mother-in-law; a person's enemies will be the members of his own household."
Mt 10:34-35

126

"Anyone who finds his life will lose it; anyone who loses his life for my sake will find it."
Mt 10:39

131

"'Again, the kingdom of Heaven is like a merchant looking for fine pearls; when he finds one of great value he goes and sells everything he owns and buys it.'"
Mt 13:45

136

"'In truth I tell you, if your faith is the size of a   140
mustard seed you will say to this mountain,
'Move from here to there,' and it will move;
nothing will be impossible for you."
Mt 17:20

"'I must proclaim the good news of the kingdom   142
of God to the other towns too, because that is
what I was sent to do.'"
Lk 4:42

"Be compassionate just as your Father is   147
compassionate. Do not judge, and you will not be
judged; do not condemn, and you will not be
condemned; forgive, and you will be forgiven.
Give, and there will be gifts for you: a full
measure, pressed down, shaken together, and
overflowing, will be poured into our lap; because
the standard you use will be the standard used for
you."
Lk 6: 36-38

"And that is why the Wisdom of God said, 'I will send them prophets and apostles; some they will slaughter and persecute, so that this generation will have to answer for every prophet's blood that has been shed since the foundation of the world, from the blood of Abel to the blood of Zechariah, who perished between the altar and the Temple.' Yes, I tell you, this generation will have to answer for it all."
Lk 11:49-51

Foreword

This book is dedicated to those who love Jesus but do not yet have the path to follow His Words, nor walk in His Footsteps. There have been a lot of people in my life who say they love Jesus, yet somehow, like the seed that falls by the wayside, do not embrace His words to make their lives a reflection of Him Who saved us by dying on the Cross.

My reflections are my own and are more practical than they are related to any theological teaching. You are free to use these words of mine, how I see Jesus' life and words and deeds, and use them in your own life. My intention is to be an interpreter of Jesus' Words in the Bible, with the sole purpose of giving the reader the ideas with which to make Jesus their Role Model. For in His own words, "Follow Me." (Reference, John1:43). So it is with his Apostles, and so with His saints and with those who have gone before us to meet Jesus in Heaven.

I have been raised a Catholic and learned about my faith

through Catholic school and from Sunday Masses. My attention to the readings in the Mass are mostly what I have in my memory and the homilies are tied into those but I do not profess to have a degree in theology. I have been a Secular Franciscan but due to life changes, I have asked to be excused as lapsed. In other words, I've been raised a believer and still believe that Jesus is My Savior, and He is yours too. If you but follow His words and walk in His footsteps.

My essays are all about Jesus' words in the New Testament. I reference the New Jerusalem Bible in my book. I also share experiences when they are relevant to the passages in the Bible that I write about. I think that life has its ups and downs, and it really must be emphasized that without Jesus, I would not be alive today. God, our Heavenly Father, has given us His only Son because He loves us so much that He wants Us all to go to Heaven and share in the Heavenly Banquet and to experience the riches that only Heaven can give. Life on earth is not where we are destined to stay. We go through our individual lives and through each event, or moment, whether alone or with our friends, family or coworkers, God talks to us in a million different ways. It is for us to ponder on these events and find some connection with God. Jesus, His Son, dwelt amongst us as a human being and went through life just like anyone of us. And He suffered through it and went through His Calvary and carried His cross. We too, must go through our Calvary and carry our cross and strive to be Like Jesus, so that We can rise up one day and become a heavenly soul.

In conclusion, think of my book as a way to ease the day's burden – you can read the chapters in any order and think about how the content can relate to what you might have experienced or what someone in your family may be going through. I think a lot of people want to love Jesus, to love His words, to do what He wants us to do. Some of them, maybe more than some, can't go through that process. Something or someone is hindering their growth in Jesus. What is important then, is that this obstacle be removed so that more growth – in the form of Grace – can take place and finally, we all find ourselves walking the walk – following Jesus and gaining heaven.

I wish you all the blessings of the Holy Spirit in your life's journey.

Mary A Faderan

Chapter One

The next day, after Jesus had decided to leave for Galilee, he met Philip and said, "Follow Me"

Jn 1:43

St. Francis of Assisi told his followers that they all must follow in the footsteps of Jesus. In this way, we too must follow in the footsteps of Jesus because He was the first to go to Heaven after His earthly life was finished.

For those who think that follow in Jesus's footsteps is easy, let us think again. It was a lot for Jesus to live through thirty-three years of life. He started his ministry at the age of thirty and got into trouble with the Jews.

For those like me, who didn't get this until I joined the Secular Franciscans, it became abundantly clear that following Jesus in His footsteps was not going to be easy. As a Secular Franciscan, I was given the task of reading the Gospel and finding ways in it to be a follower of Jesus. I tried and tried and failed a lot. I was living a life of a career woman, intent on getting to the top, or maybe management where I would be enjoying the perks of that rung in the ladder. So, following Jesus' footsteps was probably not something anyone going up the ladder of success was thinking of doing. I was probably less eager to go up the ladder, though, as I kept up with my vocation as a Franciscan. The lessons from our monthly meetings were good and kept us all aware that Francis was a true saint, totally selfless, and even to the point of giving his clothes away. In my own life, the career trajectory went out the window after a while. I cared more for my family life than going off on business trips, training sessions, and also became more aware of the fake attitudes of those who wanted to get to the top. Now, not everyone was like that in my experience, but it was obvious that if one wanted to become successful in business, they had to give up some of their sincerity, their genuineness, and their family time.

However, as much as I could to keep up with the Franciscan way, it just was a challenge. I remember asking St Francis how do I keep up with following Jesus in my life when I sometimes dozed at night instead of praying the evening prayers? How could someone in this professed faith keep to being honest, find time to give to others, go to the bingo games that we held for the mentally ill patients twice a year, and things that had to do with Franciscanism.

So, I decided before anything else, to read the Gospels more, and study Jesus' words. How did He think and what made Him say these things?

I decided after reading Jesus' words that He is a POET. I mean, He is. Poets aren't immediately connected with the Bible, although the Bible is considered a literary work by the secular literary crowd. But He is a Poet. When you read His words, consider how they symbolically give meaning to You as a person. If you think of the words "Follow me" that He said to Phillip, it seemed as though He only said it as a throwaway line. Come and follow me, I'll be your leader. A lot of us are followers of leaders. In corporate or other milieus, there are the leaders and there are the followers. But, when it comes down to it, when Jesus tells YOU to Follow Him, it is a significant command. It is a command that means YOU need to follow what He says, what he does and what He means.

I will be giving more examples of Jesus' poetic words later as we go along. But keep it in mind, and there will be a revelation to You that Jesus was more than a leader and more than someone in history. He really was and is the Son of God. He was and is God and Man. He was and is THE ONE AND ONLY Savior of Souls.

Each of us has a soul, and that is something a lot of us don't think about much. You might think souls are dusty old things; souls are not dusty, and they are a true reflection of You as God's own creation. When Jesus looks at You, He sees your soul. A lot of those whom I listened to at Mass or during a talk mention that we each of us have to reflect Jesus. For you to reflect Jesus, You must become Jesus. It is there that You need to understand that following Jesus will make You a reflection of Him because You finally know what His Words are all about. Life will be hard on your soul. It will make it dim, and yes, dusty. It will throw a lot of bad things at your soul so that you can barely lift up your head and gaze up at the sky to see the beauty of nature and the chirping of birds. You won't see the snow as beautiful but as a nuisance to your morning commutes. You won't see babies as humans but as blobs.

Chapter Two

"Jesus answered, 'Destroy this Temple, and in three days I will raise it up."

Jn 2:19

The real story of Jesus's Resurrection is a template for us as humans on earth. We don't really die and get resurrected every day of the week, but we do go through a process of death. Death can mean getting an injury on the job or doing the gardening or something like a passing sort of thing. You don't really die, but you experience a part of death. The tissue bleeds, there is pain, and you go for a bandage and then it becomes all new again. Or, in terms of the mind, one goes through death by being emotionally upset by someone who mocks you for your beliefs, because you are rejected by a college, or because you get ditched by a boyfriend or girlfriend.

In my experience, Jesus's death and resurrection is played over and over again through my life's milestones. I once tried to get into medical school and when the letters rejecting me arrived, I was totally devastated. I cried for two days and then on the third day, I was over it. See what I mean? I got to the third day and somehow, I recovered and fought to live another day, another lifetime, another career.

Jesus' poetry is seen here. He doesn't mean the Temple where the big commotion He causes happens. It means, His Body. He was making a prediction that He will die and then He will be raised from the dead.

I once attended a class given by a professor of Philosophy. He looked like Jesus actually. The greying hair and beard notwithstanding. I think if Jesus lived to that age He would look like him. My professor, I'll call him Dr. Ryan, made us think of depression. He taught us about light and dark. Chiaroscuro. The Descartesian idea of the mind being superior to the body. He said that with this type of duality, we cannot be whole. He mentioned how the Indians (Native American) were more wholistic in their view of their beliefs – their humanity. I was pretty impressed and figured that was something important. I kind of digress here but only to say that there are a lot of philosophical things that we need to be cautious of. Sometimes, the simplest things are the most important to take to heart.

Dr. Ryan went on about depression, something that I had suffered for a long time after losing a loved one. At that time, years before I ever knew this loved one, Dr. Ryan said that when you are depressed, you need to dive into it. Just enter it wholly and let it sink into your existence. Let the darkness surround you and study it, make it something that you can find a truth in. Why are you depressed? What makes you depressed? There are some who are depressed by withdrawing into themselves. Some are not like that, they express it by acting out. In my case, my depression was to withdraw, to stay in a dark room, to think or maybe not to think. Yet, Dr. Ryan said, you enter the depression accepting it and then you master it by knowing what caused it, why you got that way, and what you could do about it in the future. In many cases, depression is going to stay around, mainly because there are melancholic types of people. That is something that goes with the personality types. For those who get that way, it is really a way to get into a dialogue with God. When you're depressed, it might always be because of external situations, people who tune you out, or people who leave you and don't give a damn anymore about you. There are so many causes of depression, of course. The ones that people seem to have a problem with is when they are in a major depressive episode and then the medical people have to intervene in order to prevent a big problem. I think that is another set of circumstances that I might not be able to truly explain. What makes a major episode what it is? It might be that it is an accumulation of a series of minor depressive episodes, where there is no light and there is no hope.

I'm trying to say that depression is pretty hard to understand or get into without a lot of guidance. If you must see somebody then please do. I think that if You were to talk to God, as Jesus always did and He went to the top of the mountains to pray, then the chances of your getting out of the depression are better. I can't tell you what you should do, but I am giving an example of what a philosophy professor discussed.

I've been in a major depressive situation, but thanks to God, I now am happy and whole. I feel as though going through all that, the hospitals, the years of talk therapy, the medications, and the whole atmosphere of being with other patients who were on different medications – those were so profoundly moving to me. I still can tell when a person is on some sort of medication. The symptoms are there. For those who are feeling as though they can't get out of this, I have to tell you that you will someday. But the meds may have to continue. There are a lot of those who are normal and live and drive semi-trucks that are on medications for depression. And they are fine. The whole metabolic problems that mental illness can cause have been regulated.

For Jesus to heal you, You need to talk to Him every day, every time you feel sad and depressed. It is very important. Remember the story of the Crucifixion and Resurrection.

Archbishop Sheen once said that the Agony in the Garden was a metaphor for mental illness. Imagine how Jesus felt when He knew that His Hour was near. He asked God if He could pass on the cup of suffering. But He got up and took his apostles out of their slumber and faced the soldiers who came to take him away.

Let Jesus' suffering be a comfort to you. He suffered for ALL of us. He suffered the WORST things, the WORST and most BRUTAL and CRUEL humiliations and hurts. He died for our sins. And HE KNEW WHAT YOU WOULD BE GOING THROUGH. This is a comfort to me, because when there were times when I was upset about something in my life, there was that Crucifix in my room where I contemplated that – yes, Jesus did go through it the worst than I ever will.

One more thing. Our bodies are the Temples of the Holy Spirit. When anyone wants to destroy your Spirit, then that is when You need Jesus with You. It is said that the Devil hates it when You call on Jesus' name. I think you should always keep Jesus near to you whenever you feel threatened in a very subtle but significant way. There are a LOT of people who go through tremendous torture from unseen forces and many of them are not aware that calling on Jesus to be with them will free them of these forces. In the current environment of this world, the forces of Evil and the Culture of Death are what makes people depressed, sick, suicidal and homicidal. The terrorists are out there, but they may even be unseen by the normal human being. Therefore, we must always keep our bodies as pure as they can be. Seek out the Lord and ask Him to help you to purify your souls and your bodies as well. The Sacrament of Reconciliation is a great Sacrament. You need to confess what is in your heart that caused problems in you and between you and somebody else. Once you have those problems released from you, then the Grace of the Holy Spirit will return to you and dwell in you.

Those who feel as though they cannot have this Sacrament because they don't belong to a Catholic Church, you should seek out a clergyman who can listen to you and give you a way to become free from the shackles of sin. The shackles of sin are those that Satan puts over you and makes you his slave.

At the very least, you need to go somewhere where it's calm and peaceful, go somewhere that is safe and non-threatening and then, like Jesus on the mountain, call upon Him and tell Him your sins. I am sure that He will come to You and give you peace of mind. I think that those who feel that they can't get to a priest, to are not in any denomination or church, that they will be able to do this and find peace. The other thing that might be of help is to do something good for another, and not let anyone else know what you did. In that way, you are actually doing penance, and you are helping lift up somebody else to Jesus.

Chapter Three

"Simon Peter answered, 'Lord, to whom shall we go? You have the message of eternal life, and we believe; we have come to know that you are the Holy One of God.'

Jn 6:68-69

In this scene from John's Gospel, some of Jesus' followers left Him because Jesus was speaking of His Body and Blood as the means to have eternal life. So Jesus asks those who have remained whether they too, should leave Him. And Peter's answer spoke to me.

Without Jesus, we are really lost souls. I know this is not Jesus' words, but it is something that I feel should be discussed. We are born in this world, and if we are lucky, we are baptized in the Spirit and in Truth. We must always cling to Jesus wherever and whenever we think of it – the Spirit in us prays to God so that we humans can communicate with Him and His Son.

I know that in life's experiences, we have so many things and people we set our hopes on. We hope that our husbands and wives will be the ones to get us out of trouble, to get us to the Promised Land (whatever that may be at the moment), and to make us better than we are. We strive to impress them, to make them proud of us. And that is good up to a point. If we have chosen a good spouse, then making them want to be proud of us will help us to be better than we are. If our spouses are not perfect (nobody is, really, right?) we end up trying to please somebody who can be vain, shallow, prone to anger, bullying, abusive and everything that's bad. In our jobs, we hope that we can place our hopes that they will always be there. But these days, jobs are transitory more often than not. So it is really important to place our trust in Jesus for He is the Way, the Truth and the Life.

There's the parable in the bible about a man who puts his house on shaky ground, and the waters of the sea come up in a storm to break it down. That's what I mean about putting yourself and your soul in the hands of those who aren't strong like Jesus is. Jesus IS STRONG. He has conquered Death. If you think of it, how awesome that HE DID CONQUER DEATH. Death has no more the threat to You as a person than anything else.

Why be afraid to die? The other side of death is God Who will be welcoming His children, You, hopefully.

I think that if you placed your trust in Jesus' strength and power, you will be always coming up on top. Not on top of the material world. But like the cat who falls from a height, he lands on his feet all the time. So will You land on your feet IF you put your trust in Jesus. Ask Him to help you to find the right person to marry, to give you children that will be a blessing instead of a curse, to give you a home that is sacred and filled with love and laughter, a vehicle that will be modest and yet have a long life. I know that these are material things, but God is the Bounty of All Riches and Wealth. I don't mean everything that's expensive, glamorous, bling-y and in the fashion magazines. I mean the real and true wealth that only comes from God, from the One Who knows what we need.

There's so much to say about the Bounty of God. It is a Gift of grace, of good sense, of a straight thought, of kind words, of happiness in the face of fear and impending sorrow. We cannot always predict when or where, but we can always be assured of Jesus' love for Us. We are His adopted brothers and sisters. He told his grieving Mother the Virgin Mary on the cross that she was now the mother of John, and in this he meant the mother of us all.

That is why I think of Jesus as a poet-God or God-poet. There is a wealth of meaning and symbolism in His words. It is always a treasure to find something that speaks to you when you read the Gospels.

Chapter Four

"Do not be judging according to appearances; let your judgement be according to what is right."

Jn 7:24

In this time as in times past, the appearance of people figures highly in a lot of things. A beautiful woman will always have a date on Saturday night, and be assured of a marriage before she turns the age of thirty (or twenty-two, these days). A handsome man will be assured of a high paying job, unless he has a problem with his speech, and will probably shoot up to the top of the corporate ladder in a very short amount of time. I don't think this is at all debatable. The last position I held was in a corporate office setting and I was struck by the number of women who looked good, had no weight problems and always got promoted. The men were the same, but mostly successful because they were trained to look smart and be smart and talk smart. I don't mean to begrudge people for their looks. There are many smart and beautiful people who are genuinely nice.

What I'm getting at is that beauty fades and then one has to figure out what will keep them from being lost in the past, finding themselves without a rudder or place in the world. I once was in a congregation where the priest mentioned meeting an old friend from college. His friend confessed that he had undergone a change of perspective. His friend said that he judged people by their exterior appearances and not on their inner qualities. The priest was gratified to hear this as I was. I too, was struck by appearances. An old friend from school also told me that people think that a beautiful person is always good, and that isn't so. I think that to me, as I write this, I feel as though God is telling me that I have that fault.

It is a fault ingrained in a lot of us, who grow up in a society where beauty is prized and success follows beauty. It is still something I struggle with, and sometimes I fail. But, I think that knowing one's faults is the start of being saved – by God, by the Spirit, and by Jesus. The words of Jesus says to judge according to what is right. I suppose one should not judge others at all, because God is the final judge. However, I think that we ought not to judge wrongly in terms of what a person we behold before us is like based on their appearance.

In my mind, whenever a person I meet is attractive, the attraction is going to have to include the expression in their eyes and the sincerity of their smile. Moreover, an attractive person to me may not even be all about their physical attributes, but because they have a sense of humour, a way of looking at life that is wise and full of gratitude. I no longer look at the fashionable clothes in the magazines these days – except to check whether the styles are still sensible. One needs to be better than what they look like and it is sad to see people fall for the wrong person based on their perception that that person will be as good as they look.

The magazines that I mention have all the same agenda – to promote beauty and perfection. The many plastic surgeons that advertise online and in these same magazines are evidence that the current world meme is to be a good as money can buy. Advertisers are eager to put up the latest in makeup, fashion, cars and houses. These are the trappings of a lost soul, or a soul that has stopped listening to God. What is more appalling is that there are these beautiful people who ensnare unknowing and naïve young people to be like them and forsake the real beauty that they have inside. For the most important thing, as I mentioned above, is that the Soul is where beauty lies and what Jesus reads when You call His name. There are so many other ways to be beautiful. Sometimes being a little different in appearance will help your character and make you grow into a wise and more attractive person.

Chapter Five

"If you ask me anything in my name, I will do it. If you love me, you will keep my commandments."

Jn 14:14-15

A lot of times this passage doesn't get enough attention. But this is really where it's at. You can always ask Jesus what you would like for Him to do to You and for You; and, if you love Him you will always be sure to keep His commandments.

When I was a teenager, I didn't go out late with my friends. I always made sure that if I ever went to a party (which wasn't a lot of the time, but it happened a few times) that I called my parents and told them I was on my way home and got home early enough so that the sun had not yet set. In those days, I was very much loved and I very much loved my parents. I told myself that I would never do anything to make them worry about me or my safety. I went with people they trusted and then whenever there were any school dances, I went with friends that my parents knew and trusted. I was very much an obedient child, and maybe that is one reason why I wasn't a popular kid. I wasn't "outgoing" enough, to quote my professor of chemistry. That was my reputation, and I don't care if anyone didn't want to be friends with me for that reason.

So with this passage, I think that we should take care to be obedient to Jesus' commandments IF we love Him. Love is an act of the will, I am told. But love comes naturally when one feels they are cherished. Cherished by their Creator, by their Savior, by their parents and family. I think that loving Jesus is a prerequisite to being saved, to gaining Heaven.

The commandments are not hard to follow. One must always adore God and love God. One must never utter an oath and one must always honor their parents. It is a sin to steal, to want someone's goods and someone's spouse. It is a sin to kill and to go after what doesn't belong to you. You should always honor the Lord's Day and keep it sacred.

I remember how some prayer groups that I belonged to would, after prayers were said (like the Rosary), set up a poker game. It never ceased to amaze me how they would willingly say prayers to Jesus and his Mother, and pledge to love them always and lead good lives, yet they would at a drop of a hat, sit at a poker table and gamble. I felt as though it was a great sin, and of course, because it was at a residence, maybe I was over reacting. But it felt wrong to me and to this day, I feel that way. I have since left those groups and I hope they have either given up the prayer group or given up the gambling. It would be to their salvation if they gave up the latter and resolved never to combine prayer and gambling. Do the casinos in Las Vegas have a chapel in their midst? I have never gone to a casino so I do not know. But I surely hope that no chapel is inside a casino.

Chapter Six

"I am the true vine, and my Father is the vinedresser. Every branch in me that bears no fruit he cuts away, and every branch that does bear fruit he prunes to make it bear even more."

Jn 15:1-2

This passage is a meaningful one to me. My mother considered her symbol to be the vine, because she was so much filled with love for Jesus and His Mother. The pruning of the vine, similar to the pruning of a life, is meant to make that vine, that person, more fruitful.

How many people do you know who have lost a loved one, or lost a job or lost property? It isn't all by chance. Nothing is really a coincidence. It hurts yes, but then one needs to look at it in the perspective of Jesus' poetry. I know that loss is hard on one's life, but when you consider what happened to Job, and how he bore it with great patience, uttering that God was a Good and Merciful God, then it makes sense. Job came through the many problems God gave him with such grace that God gave him a whole lot more than what he used to have.

So we must try to look at loss as what Job would say – The Lord gives and The Lord takes away, Glory be to God. In the midst of loss, God wants us to know that He is eager to hear your voice and ask for His mercy, for

His forgiveness, for His Grace.

Once I was in a crisis at a part of my life when I failed in a job I had. It caused a lot of hurt in a family and that incident went out of my memory for years and would have been forgotten except for a momentary vision that I had when I was driving down the road. So, I was totally terrified that I had lost God's protection and ran to a priest to confess my omission. I think that when the priest realized that this was something I needed to have forgiveness, he prayed over me and then said in a kind voice, that out of bad comes good with God's help. He assured me that God sees all from His perspective with no reference to Time. And, so He can go back to that particular part of my life and bless that event and make something good come from it.

So, we cannot say that when something bad happens in

our lives that that's it. No. When something bad happens, it is an opportunity for you to call God to be a witness to what happened and to take it and make it better for your future. It is the intent of the Devil to shackle you what bad thing you might have done in the past, to throw it at you every time you think of something reminding you of it, and to keep your future in his hands. The idea of Calling God to dispel the Devil's curse is of primary importance. You must never give up on God no matter how bad things are going in your life. That quote that says: "When a door closes, God opens a window," is something that I think applies in a general way. God will bless you for going through suffering and if you confess to Him whatever thing you might have done, whatever responsibility you might have omitted doing, or for leaving something undone – He will forgive and make it all right.

Chapter Seven

"If the world hates you, you must realize that it hated me before it hated you. If you belonged to the world, the world would love you as its own; but because you do not belong to the world, because my choice of you has drawn you out of the world, that is why the world hates you."

Jn 15:18-19

This passage has always been a comfort to me. In my

later years as an employee, I got into a heap of trouble at work with my more modern thinking coworkers. Facebook was at its prime. There were all friends who wanted to show how great their lives were, how much they possessed, how great their vacations were – all for a chance to show it on Facebook. I still have Facebook but I use it for my business.

In those days, and still now, I was vocal against abortion and against gay marriage. I didn't really spout off at work or anything like that. But one time a gay colleague made a post about being pro-gay marriage. I commented that I hope to still be friends with him despite his views but I was personally opposed to gay marriage.

I also posted on Facebook a lot of anti-abortion pictures, or pro-life events, and made it clear there that I supported the culture of life.

That time marked the end of my career as an employee. My coworkers shunned me. They didn't care to listen to me when I spoke in meetings. They keyed my car. Twice, maybe three times. They made it clear that I was not their friend anymore. I was written up once, my boss humiliated me in front of a conference room filled with people, and I was totally alone. I got transferred to another department and endured the marginalization until I decided to retire early.

So how does this passage make sense to my story? It just means that when You are with Jesus, and You believe in His Commandments and are one of His friends, then You are going to be frequently derided, hated, and even killed for what you profess to believe in. I have not been killed yet and I live to fight another day each day the sun rises over my bedroom window.

The life of a friend of Jesus is going to be like that. For me, being a solitary witness for Jesus means it is all a piece. I don't mind that those people did these things to me and my career. It was probably time to leave and God just made it a quicker exit. If you think you need friends like these people, then you need to have your head examined. Friends are hard to find if You are a friend of Jesus's. The friends you have would have to be aware that being your friend will make them a moving target. If this is too harsh a statement, so be it. The life on earth is at a place where there are lines in the sand. Either you are For Jesus or You are For Satan.

There is a light at the end of this tunnel. Heaven. You need to be aware that life is transitory. Heaven can really exist in your life if You have friends of Jesus in it. These people are gone from my everyday life. You really ought not to find good friends at work. If you need friends, you can always pick up a book by Fulton Sheen or Ignatius of Loyola, or Pope Benedict. Their words will make you feel at peace and then life will be better. God rewards His friends with a lot of grace and a lot of happiness. You just need to be strong, courageous, and be willing to fight for your place in God's family.

Chapter Eight

"I have told you all this so that you may find peace in me. In the world you will have hardship but be courageous. I have conquered the world."

Jn 16:33

This passage is a corollary to the previous one. It means that in Jesus you will find Peace. Jesus went through His Calvary and so will we all. But He conquered it all by rising from the dead and coming to the Father. So will we all have our resurrection and we will be given our just reward.

Chapter Nine

"Jesus replied, 'You would have no power over me at all if it had not been given you from above.'"

Jn 19:11

Can you get in to this passage? How does this apply to your life as a worker? How do you feel when your boss makes you feel like a fool or gives you a ton of work just an hour before quitting time? How does it make you feel when you have a boss from Hell?

I have to admit that my bosses, most of them, were really nice people. But still with each job I had there was work to do and even though I disliked doing some things, I had to think that this is part of being a human being, a worker, a part of society, of a culture where one earns a wage.

Jesus was a human to all who didn't see Him as God. Pilate was the man who ordered his flogging. Being human meant that Jesus had to submit to what all humans had to go through to – well, get by or, in His case, to get handed over to someone worse. And get crucified.

We all as humans heard the phrase "She will crucify you!" to someone who was going to get punished for screwing up a project or whatever. Crucifixion exists in this world. It's not a physical one. It's just as hard to endure, if you are a human being.

So for me, I had to think of this passage when I had a difficult day and couldn't exactly talk back to my supervisor. In those days, I had to keep my feelings under control, to keep my mouth shut, so I wouldn't lose my job. I had a family, bills to pay, a house to pay off – things that kept me (and a lot of others like me) tied to my job.

I have to think of what Jesus, King of the Universe, Royal Son of the Father, had to endure at the hands of those who would (if they could really see themselves through the eyes of God) only be the size of a snail's butt. If Jesus could be that tough to take that kind of abuse, then we should be also tough like Him. And we should be humble because we are but the means to saving this world. We need to be humble because we cannot imperil the lives of those who are innocent – our spouses, our children, our mothers and fathers. So we must be always that way because Jesus was like that. Our Role Model.

Chapter Ten

"And Jesus said to them: 'Come after me and I will make you fishers of people.'"

Mk 1:17

This passage is a famous one, and it definitely shows Jesus' poetic nature and, his humorous side. The first time this metaphor – fishers of people – came to my consciousness was the movie "The Shoes of the

Fisherman" which was a great movie but in truth, I don't have much a recollection of the story except that it was about the Pope. But the phrase was catchy and I fully believe that Jesus did make his apostles into great fishers of men.

There are many who say that the apostles were unformed when they first got the call from Jesus. They received their formation, or training, while they sat at Jesus' feet as He preached the Gospel to everyone who went to listen to him speak. This experience was very valuable to them once Jesus rose to Heaven on Ascension Day, and they were given more strength and courage when the Holy Spirit descended upon them on Pentecost.

I think that as followers of Jesus, we too, are given the gifts to b 'fishers' of men. Not in the same way perhaps as the clergy or the Pope but as witnesses for Jesus. We bring our families and friends and coworkers to Jesus in our daily prayers and tell Him how they are. One or two times we get a request from people to pray for them or their loved one who might be in need to extra help in their lives. So, we all help in 'casting' the net, unknowingly or not.

You might think that this sort of act is a radical thing. It is, but it isn't it true that when we gather at our dinner table we let each other know of the news from our own little world? For example, when one's wife tells him of an experience she had at the grocery store, or at work – isn't that something like bringing our experiences to the authority figure in our lives – the head of the family? The same when our parents asked us how school was and sometimes we tell them of an event, a scheduled trip to an historic place or just a small scuffle at the schoolyard between a bully and an unlucky target.

So we do the same when we bring these sorts of stories, experiences and events to Jesus in prayer. We also bring the latest in the world to Him and how these changes that are in store for our communities and the larger society we live in might affect us. In many countries, especially now, there is a great upheaval that concerns the economy of the European Union or the state of the United Kingdom (called Brexit). In these places, don't the citizens have concerns and where do they bring their concerns but to their immediate authorities. Can they not also bring these concerns in prayer to God and His Son? It is not only the immediate need or the nearest councilman that needs to be implored. These people are still human, swept to and fro in their thinking by their own weaknesses. If God were to be implored, as Jesus sought Him in Prayer, then the power of the Most High will bend its gaze upon our world and our environment to effect REAL change. Change that will astound and make you gasp in wonder. "Why didn't I ask Him sooner?"

To those who still aren't convinced, try it out and then keep it going. There is that parable again of the persistent woman who asks the judge to listen to her case and he finally gives in and gives her the justice she asks for. Is it not the same? We ask our mothers to give us something we want and nag them until they give it. I remember this happen with me when I was small and it goes on in every household. The KEY is to be persistent and ask always. God works in His own time and in His own way. To be persistent, to be patient, and to WAIT UPON THE LORD is what works and it is going to work every single time.

The troubles of this world are depending on our casting

the net in order to be eased or removed and our societies' ills will be a thing of the past. Not all of them might be removed at the same time, but God is ever so Wise that He makes things better for the good of all.

Chapter Eleven

"And he replied, 'Who are my mother and my brothers?' And looking at those sitting in a circle around him, he said, 'Here are my mother and my brothers. Anyone who does the will of God, that person is my brother and sister and mother.'"

Mk 3:33-35

I once met a woman who complained asking what exactly was the 'will of God' to those who were in her company. I said nothing because at the time, I wasn't sure what it was. I had heard of God's will all the time in growing up and throughout Sunday Mass homilies and then when people in my circle of friends discussed it. Usually, it was associated with something happening that one could not countermand. "Oh, it's God's will that so-and-so died." And then my Mother passed away and I felt as though it was the end of my life as I knew it. I railed against God and pleaded with Him to let her stay longer with me. But she passed away and is now in a better place – in God's bosom. So, for me, the will of God is implacable. Something all of us who believe in God have to cooperate with, if not, accept.

When Jesus asked in the Garden of Gethsemane whether the 'cup' should pass from his lips, He too was asking about God's will for Him to die on the Cross. It was to be and Jesus went through it and He came back to life even stronger and more powerful. He now sits at God's Right Hand to deliver the judgment to the living and the dead.

What is to be taken away from the cooperation with God's will then? We pray for Mercy and ask Him to help us in all ways that He might want. Prayers that start out with a petition should always include "if it should be Your Will" in it. But we also plead His Mercy in our prayers because we all know that we are worthless in the eyes of God. We are His children, yes, but we are here to serve Him as people who must help in the transformation of this world so that more will be saved, more will be given His merciful graces.

In a prayer to the Virgin Mother, we say, "Hail our life, our sweetness and hope, in this vale of tears..." This is a prayer that gives me a bittersweet feeling. We are all subject to God's Will and we all live in a valley of tears. None of us are exempt. We are happy, then we are sad, and we weep for many things, and so the only way to have comfort is to petition God that He might look upon our lives and see how miserable we are without His Presence.

It is misery that makes it clear that God is missing in our lives. Were God to be with Us, we would be happy in the middle of misfortune. I always think of a picture of children, teen boys, playing basketball in the wreckage of their playground in the Philippines, smiling at the camera, right after the huge typhoon that flattened many cities and towns in that country. I wonder at how they managed to smile, to even play basketball, and to gather together to be children still. I think God was present there with them. There is that feeling in children, mostly, of being happy playing with even the simplest of toys. That is because God is with them all the time. It is our duty as parents and aunts and uncles and grandparents to keep our children uppermost in our minds when pleading with God. Children, as Jesus said, are the first ones to get to Heaven, and I think it's because Heaven is with them still.

When babies are born, and you watch them smiling in their sleep, it seems not to make sense. But they are likely given a moment's grace from their Holy Angels. This is most reassuring.

So, we must be like the children of this world, be happy and hope and have confidence in God that He will take care of us no matter how dire it might look.

Chapter Twelve

"And some seeds fell on rich soil, grew tall, and strong, and produced a good crop; the yield was thirty, sixty, even a hundredfold.' And he said, 'Anyone who has ears for listening should listen.'"

Mk 4:8-9

This is part of the story of the sower and the seed. There are the different people depicted as those who have varying ways of receiving God's word. The seed falls on the edge of the path and birds came to eat them up. Some seed falls on rocky ground and found it hard to grow so they withered away. And then seed fell on rich soil and grew to a hundredfold. Jesus then finishes the parable with the words "Anyone who has ears for listening should listen."

I think this parable is a famous one and every year when this is read in Mass, it is always a heartening story for everyone. Still, not everyone really sees how it might apply in their lives. Their ears aren't primed to hear God's word. They have a lot on their minds. They were late to Mass and their minds are still dwelling on how little Suzy kept them all waiting. Or, they are looking forward to the football game later that day and whose team was playing whom. Or, they have fallen asleep in front of the priest who is delivering the homily and cannot hear at all.

How do we prevent this lack of hearing, lack of listening

from happening when God's voice calls us? I think it's a difficult question. There is a saying that God will listen to the prayers of a soul even if the prayers are said in a jumble or lacking in fervor. You wish you were the person at the front of the church bowed in prayer and eyes closed and praying silently. But that is a rare occurrence, from my experience, and sometimes we all get a little distracted in different ways.

What's important is to remember what the Gospel of the day (Sunday) is when we are in our cars ready to get out of the parking lot and motoring off to have lunch somewhere. If we can remember the Gospel at that moment, then we will be assured we will remember it all day and maybe the following week. I think that is true, and we should test ourselves. What is it that the priest said? What lesson did we learn that Sunday? How do we apply it to our everyday lives? How do we become the rich and fertile soil that Jesus is looking to plant His grace?

Some people take notes during Mass and that is fine. I have taken notes at conferences where there is an esteemed speaker of the faith on the podium. But do I really look at these notes afterwards when everyone's gone home? No. It isn't like we are going to be quizzed later in a pop exam. But maybe we are quizzed at some point where a situation comes smack into our lives to challenge our faith. How strong is it and how much love do we have for Jesus? There are many who are challenged and come out of it bereft of their souls. Some are luckier and they keep their friendship with Jesus intact.

A young man I worked with once said that God tests everyone throughout their lives. I felt a bit scared by that statement – almost like "Doesn't God trust me to get it right the first time?" was my unspoken response. Yet God does test us time and time again. He tests our faith, how much we can endure under the focus of His gaze, how we can keep on loving Him no matter how hard it might be.

We love Him in all the people we meet, or at least, we should aim to. We can't always be effusive in loving people, strangers or ones who are from a different culture. But we must see them with the eyes of Jesus. We must have Jesus in our thoughts to discern what it is we are facing. He must always be IN us and WITH us when we encounter challenges and tests.

It is also here that we must decipher whether it is the Evil one that tests us. Remember the time when Jesus was challenged by Satan in the desert. It is important to make sure that God is always present in our lives, every second of the day. It is that crucial. Otherwise we will fall, and one day, we may not be able to get up.

Chapter Thirteen

"And if any place does not welcome you and people refuse to listen to you, as you walk away shake off the dust under our feet as evidence to them."

Mk 6:11

There is a similar passage that goes the other way – where Jesus tells his apostles to give their peace to those whose house they stay in and if their peace is refused then it will come back to them.

We all have experienced this alienation in our lives –

where we join a group or even move to a new community and there is nothing there but hostility or indifference. So we have to say it is them and not us. We shake the dust off them as we leave never to return. We can't always keep trying to be a part of what is not meant for us. That is where our persistence will lead us astray.

Teens and young career minded people are prone to this sort of treatment. They want to join the "IN Crowd" and be popular like the leaders. They join fraternities, and they join country clubs and they join the best and most bodacious athletic groups. They take up sports that only make their bodies die slowly in the hopes of slimming down or looking hip.

You must read between the lines and see the writing on the wall in these places. If you don't like how it feels, no matter how you think they are all great, you need to leave them for the air they breathe is polluted with a great deal of unhappy and selfish ideas.

It is a difficult test we all go through. Ads on TV, Facebook, Twitter, and others like them make it look so appealing – to belong, to show off, to gloat, to shame, to put down and ridicule. The suicidal tendencies are enhanced by such as these. It is so very saddening to see how kids are prey to these and become so absorbed with changing themselves to the point of becoming other than what they are – children of God, of the Spirit of God. Yet they are changed and if we don't watch for them, they become alien and they are lost.

I've talked about joining places and wanting to belong. The passage is about those places where we are ostracized and rebuffed. I think this is a difficulty when we as earnest workers are placed and hired into companies that are hostile to the charity that we have in our hearts. We all cannot choose where we work, sometimes. We have to endure a great deal of being rebuffed and put down and become sad in our nine-to-five jobs. What do we do then? We call Jesus to help. We must. Nobody in Human Resources is going to be on your side. HR is an arm of the management. Period. They give you what you need to know to get yourself insured, get yourself a paycheck and that's about it. You can ask them to look at how you are being treated by a bully of a boss, but it's still not clear whether they will take your side.

We all have to have patience. Once God intervenes in our lives, GO FOR IT. He will come and take you out of Hell and it will be much better when you have shaken the dust from the place where you were abused and used.

Daily prayer is key. Lifting your thoughts to God every time you think of Him is great.

In this passage I have the idea that Jesus foresaw what sorts of suffering His followers will go through. He went through this first. He goes before us and we know that He will be with us through thick and thin.

What I think we should do once Jesus leads us out of the desert is to THANK HIM and frequently too. It is something that He wants to hear. He needs your feedback. He wants to show you that this is His doing – rescuing you. You must acknowledge it and that will endear you to Him no end.

Chapter Fourteen

"What gain, then, is it for anyone to win the whole world and forfeit his life?"

Mk 8:36

Years ago, early in my career in a corporate milieu, I was told that if I wanted to move up in the company, my boss would help me get the proper training. I didn't say anything to him at the time and thought about it frequently. Turning it over in my mind. I thought of a lot of things that promotions would mean. Yes, it meant a better paycheck. More money to pay off bills and get the family needs attended to. Fixing the house, getting a bigger car, things like that. Then I thought about the downside. I would probably (most likely) be sent on trips to deal with business contacts, or to company meetings to discuss big company issues, lots of TUMS in my desk drawers, getting hung up to dry when a project I headed would get axed due to any reason under the sun. I also found out that I would have to sign a document where, if I ever got into legal problems for my company, that I would agree to going to jail for them if needed. The company assured those who get promoted that they would have their back.

Baloney.

You know how it is nowadays. People are squealing on their former employers, their best buddies, in order to escape jail time. In order to escape fines and all kinds of Hell.

It's a nice thing to be, some say, to be a manager, or supervisor or even to become a CEO. Well, I'm not into herding cats and I don't like managing people. There is a great amount of stress involved in moving up the corporate ladder. I think that this passage deals with this very issue. You've given up your soul to reach the very top of the heap. Is it all worth it? The money, the big mansion, the spa and pool, the collection of jewelry, the vacations to parts of the world that promise so much gratification. How about this, for example as an ad line: Buy experiences. Travel the world and buy experiences. Is that a truth? Can we buy experiences? I think they meant 'buy a vacation and experience luxury' but they've contracted the sentence and just went for the bottom line. If you can buy anything, even an experience, you've got it made, so the ad says.

I don't know whether I'm anti-wealth per se. There are many wealthy people who are generous and charitable beyond belief. But I am not sure I want to be so hugely wealthy. It is a scary thing to have wealth beyond imagination. What is wealth anyway? It's money in the bank, a brokerage account, a material thing. What if the world went into a depression? European markets take a tumble.

I'd rather have the wealth of a happy and healthy family, protected by God Himself, and forget about the inconvenience of living in a house that is in need of a few repairs. I would rather be on God's side, with my soul intact, than be on uneasy territory with a lot of sycophants who are angling to replace me in the ladder of success. It really boils down to this.

Chapter Fifteen

"For if anyone in this sinful and adulterous generation is ashamed of me and of my words, the Son of man will also be ashamed of him when he comes in the glory of his Father with the holy angels."

Mk 8:37

Once when I was shopping with my Mom in our mall, I encountered some classmates looking for a good sale. For some reason, I was embarrassed to be seen with my Mom and later, my classmates teased me for being ashamed of my own Mother in front of my friends. I think that teens have this issue and being a teenager I got suckered into feeling this way. I love my Mom dearly from birth and being ashamed of her at that point was so awful in retrospect. I don't know what made me feel ashamed, and I suppose it was just one of those things that happen to girls at that age.

It was a lesson for me, I would wager. For a future instance and it really made a dent in my consciousness. Being ashamed of your parents is a big NO-NO. No matter what they are, how little educated, or how somehow geeky, they are your parents and you must always be happy to be seen in their company. You must always be eager to introduce your friends to them. You must always give them respect, and if needed, care for them when they are sick. It is they who represent Jesus to you in many ways. They introduced You to Him when you were baptized. So to think of them as embarrassing is like shunning Jesus in order to impress the people who you would rather belong to.

Being ashamed to believe in Jesus is a sad thing. In these days where standing up for your beliefs is a big deal – yes, no matter what these beliefs may be, actually – it means a lot more if you stood up for Jesus and Who He is in your life. He gave you eternal life, and He suffered greatly for your sins.

Being like Jesus is also a good aim to have. Being like Jesus means You are a part of His Body. The Body of Jesus.

In social media, there are a lot of people who defriend those who speak out against the evils of the culture. A Facebook friend claims that she has been defriended by so many people because she spoke out against abortion. I think Facebook is the battleground where those who follow in Jesus's footsteps are tested day in and day out. It is probably best not to engage in it because sometimes there are those who like to bait people into revealing themselves as pro-life and pro-this or anti-this and then it becomes clear that the agenda behind these Facebook posts is to mark those who are followers of Jesus in order to subject them and their children to prejudice and bias in school and in the workplace.

I believe that we as followers of Jesus have to pick our battles wisely. Do not be fooled by those who want to help us to reveal our principles to strangers. It is important that we keep our families safe, and Facebook is the devil when it comes to wanting to know who you are, what you're about, where you live, who you voted for, and what sort of work you do. Keep to your principles and if you are asked, say you are a follower of

Jesus.

Chapter Sixteen

"But anyone who is the downfall of one of these little ones who have faith, would be better thrown into the sea with a great millstone hung round his neck."

Mk 9:42

This passage is Jesus's condemnation of those who pollute the innocent minds of the young, who corrupt their bodies, who lead them out of the bosom of their Families, who separate them from their husbands and wives, who kill their unborn children and who willingly throw them into slavery.

We as Jesus's followers have been marked by God as His children. Thus, the Devil is eager to find those of Jesus's friends and put them into harm's way and drag them into the sewer that he dwells in. It is a great Sin to be one of the Devil's helpers, his minions, and make a conscious act to lead them into perdition.

What do we do when this happens to our loved ones? We keep them in God by praying for them to see the light and to have the grace to turn away from sin, seek help, call home. I listened to a priest who said with a sad expression in his face, "What we need to do is to get to the basics of praying for OUR families. Forget the rest of the world. Our families are important and their salvation is what we should ask God to do." I think that was how he phrased it. It seemed like the world's so messy that it's past praying for. So all we can do now is to pray for our own people, our family members, our children. I don't know whether praying for the world will do any good, from hearing this priest's words. I guess it's gotten to the point that the evil forces have gotten to surround even the churches we attend. It's us against the devils of the world.

We hope that we can keep our young children in a cocoon of protection from what might happen in the school room, in the playgrounds, and in the day care nurseries. There's a lot of independence being thrust upon our children these days. The latch key kids. Those little kids who run home after getting off the school bus, trying to get home before anything might happen. I am both impressed and appalled that there is nobody who welcomes these kids home from school. They grow up too soon, and they might not be equipped to handle surprises. Not to mention an attack from a hostile force that no one can see.

I read in an article on The Telegraph how kids in the UK are depressed. It was a sad thing to learn. How could kids in an entire country be depressed? It means that there's something really the matter with that country if their own children are always upset, crying, unable to cope and depressed at an early age.

It's time for us to cling once more to Jesus. He is the Good Shepherd. He knows Us. He knows our children. A nation where the children are depressed, aborted at will, sexually active at an early age, prey to predators, abused and enslaved, is a nation which has gotten loose from its Jesusian moorings.

Chapter Seventeen

> "'My children.' [Jesus] said to them, 'how hard it is to enter the kingdom of God! It is easier for a camel to pass through the eye of a needle than for someone rich to enter the kingdom of God.' They were more astonished than ever, saying to one another, 'In that case, who can be saved?' Jesus gazed at them and said, 'By human resources it is impossible, but not for God, because for God everything is possible.'"
>
> Mk 10:24-27

Life is full of distractions. In my life, there were so many things to want, to get and to amount to. I once was told I was ambitious to go to a big Ivy League university for a job as a post-doctoral researcher. I felt uneasy about being called "ambitious". I went for this job and found it lacking. Everyone was a fake, it seemed to me, all those who I met and worked with. The work was also a travesty and there was every sign that the workplace was all built on a whimsical set of rules and regulations. I felt unable to get out of it, but I did, and went on with my career, such as it was. I was convinced that a great position was waiting for me, if only I went on with the path I was taking. Three times I went for different types of positions, and three times, I lost my idealism. There wasn't a place of power and influence for such as me. It seemed as though I was doomed to become an ordinary person, with an ordinary job. I had also fallen in love and that went awry. I never felt such depression as when I bade him goodbye and let him go to marry another woman. I never even felt as though I had a fighting chance to ask him to stay with me.

It is a devil of a life when what the Evil one tells you is good for you – power, money, success, the big house, the cars and all of the life you can have including the right man and smart kids – a be yours. This way of thinking is like a house of cards that falls flat on itself once you've made this thought into a shrine. There is no such world as that world if you think you have to be anyone, Somebody, to make it. That song *New York, New York* was famous when I lived in the East coast. I felt that song was almost like a beckoning. "Come to the Big Apple and be rich and famous," it said.

What does this passage tell me about life in this world? It tells me that all the efforts I made to get to a 'heaven' on this earth as some big shot in science, a part of a beautiful couple, a happy person – could ever happen to me. It takes more than that to reach the RIGHT HEAVEN that God made us to live in with Him. The whole idea of entering the kingdom of God is not based on what you own, how much money you make, and who you know on this earth. It is based on a lot of subtle things and a lot of practical things. Give your wealth away. Give yourself to God. Give Him your every thought and ask Him how you can get to his Kingdom. You will experience something akin to going through the eye of the needle – yes, I admit, I went through hell to get to the point where I could see how Jesus' words made sense. Yet, even while I was trying to climb the ladder of success, I saw who lived in each rung and I did NOT like them. They were not my type. They were all filled with ego. So much for the ladder of success. It was that realization then that made it harder to try to reach for the next rung in the ladder. At that time, God was already talking to me.

God talks to us in so many ways and through a lot of people and in the experiences you go through in life.

To have a successful life in the eyes of God is going to be a personal thing – a relationship - with Him. It'll be between Him and you. You need to understand that your life, your experiences in your life, the people in your life and family – are all tailored to fit your salvation in some way and only God can decipher it all for you. It is not for me or anyone really to say what You need to do. But read this passage and see how God is THE SOURCE of how it is possible to ENTER INTO HIS KINGDOM.

Chapter Eighteen

"In his teaching he said, 'Beware of the scribes who like to walk about in long robes, to be greeted respectfully in the market squares, to take the front seats in the synagogues and the places of honour at banquets; these are the men who devour the property of widows and for show offer long prayers. The more severe will be the sentence they receive.'"

Mk 12:38-40

My experience with those who have power and status is that they are aware, so very aware of their rank and superiority even when they try to show how very 'humble' they are. Take one of the people I used to work for – he was a big guy in the company and considered a 'great fellow' type of person. I went sometimes to a prayer group that he and his assistant organized, in order to pray for the company he headed. There were a few stragglers who came in at about 7:30 a.m. on a Friday each month, to pray and faith share. It wasn't a bad idea, but then I noticed that this 'big guy' – when it came his turn to pray – prayed knowing that he had an audience listening. I think that praying has to be something private to be really able to reach God's ears – although Jesus did say that when one or more are gathered in prayer, He will be with them.

This illustration of a highly regarded businessman in prayer may have been something that I saw as a little showy. I may be mistaken, and only God Himself can say for sure if this man was a real fake or not. It wasn't all he did in that group that made me feel like he was a show off. After all, men like these are trained to be 'on' all the time. And this was another problem that I felt a lot of corporate higher-ups had in their little bag of tricks. I saw this man in a big group of people talking, and I saw him in the small group. And in each, he scaled his show to fit the audience, but he was still talking to an audience. Not to God, but to us as an audience – to admire his piety and need to have God hear him.

Not everyone in places of power are playing to an audience. A lot of people, some presidents, even – have a real genuineness about them and they have emotions and love for their country – a lot of it shows and anyone with eyes in their head and a good heart can see for themselves and be able to figure out who is real and who isn't.

Chapter Nineteen

"A poor widow came and put in two small coins, the equivalent of a penny. Then he called his disciples and said to them, 'In truth I tell you; this poor widow has put more in than all who have contributed to the treasury; for they have all put in money they could spare, but she in her poverty has put in everything she possessed, all she had to live on.'"

Mk 12:42-44

This passage reminds me of an aunt of mine. She was the wife of a military man and had several children, all who had a lot of things they demanded of her as wife and mother. She was widowed after some time, when the children were grown or in school. Her life was unknown to me until we finally met in our town when they moved. She was a woman who prayed all the time, the beads of her rosary, and once she told me that she prayed 3,000 Hail Mary's every day. Her son seemed perplexed by this but this is another topic that is not relevant except that even her own children felt she was an anachronism.

I mention my aunt because she had the smile that made me feel so happy whenever I saw her. She always had something humourous to say. She called her children nicknames that stuck and made them feel special in their originality.

When she moved to the city as a retiree, she really had no money of her own. All that she had from whatever her husband left behind had been spent, and then she lived on a meager social security check every month.

Once, she said to me that she gave to her favorite charities – the sum of $3 in her check. It was something that made me wonder – how much work will $3 support from a widow who had no money to speak of? But, then I thought again and then I decided that this money was given to God and God would multiply it a hundred or even a thousand-fold when all was said and done.

Her life was selfless and filled with a lot of pain and suffering. Yet she loved very well. And I am sure God loved her for her widow's mite that she contributed whenever she felt she could.

Chapter Twenty

"Blessed are you when people abuse you and persecute you and speak all kinds of calumny against you falsely on my account. Rejoice and be glad, for your reward will be great in heaven; this is how they persecuted the prophets before you."

Mt 5:11-12

There is a meme these days where one has to be 'politically correct' and avoid being persecuted or tormented by those who are the 'thought police' which I think is very much a product of the culture of death.

Being a follower of Jesus means standing up for what's right in the eyes of God. What is right and what is wrong is now being obfuscated so that it makes no sense – wrong is the new right and right is the new wrong. I believe that Archbishop Sheen made this one of his tenets and I think a lot of people ought to realize that the new way of spinning bad ideas into "good" is terrible. Bad is bad and good is always good. There is no two ways about it.

Life is going to always be putting up challenges to you and your children, always giving you a hurdle and many of these are ways to see if you or your children will kowtow to those who want your obeisance. If you are shamed for believing in God, for speaking out for life, or for being a good and holy person, you must be strong and stalwart. Do not pay attention to these naysayers. Be who you are in God's eyes. Keep God in your thoughts. Help others by being a good example. Do not put anyone down, even if they are telling lies about you. Your example is proof that what these people say are lies. You can always tell a person by what they talk about: What they put down, and what their opinions are. You can always tell a fake, if you have God in your mind and heart. What you SHOULD do is to talk to God about these people and tell Him only. Do NOT talk about these liars and persecutors to anyone you don't trust. You must tell your parents or you as parents must ask your children who is, or, what is going on, to make them feel sad.

In social media, for example, many are led astray and even downright murdered or led to suicide because of their so-called Facebook "friends". It is a crime to make others look at themselves as geeks, or obese, or anything other than what they are – human beings who have a unique Self that was Thought of by God when they were formed in His likeness. It is a sad thing that Facebook is still around but a great number of people now rely on it for news, friendship and catching up with relatives around the world. I am a Facebook person too, but I don't have a lot of friends. Some of my nephews have over 700 friends, which seems overwhelming. Do YOU want seven hundred people from all over the world know what YOU are doing and saying and thinking? It's not necessary to put all sorts of things on Facebook, Twitter or LinkedIn. It's something that young people, tweens and teens tend to do and their parents must be held accountable for this. Once I saw a post a friend's daughter put on Facebook where she mentioned someone's name who was raped. Whether or not this was true, it was a BAD IDEA to post it on social media. Good for her, her parents told her to remove this post. However, that news had already gone through the newsfeeds of that girl's friends. It's that bad on social media, as if you didn't already know.

There are a lot of lies all over the place, and a lot of liars everywhere you go. The people you meet may misrepresent themselves just to be accepted, just to get a great job, and just to find someone to love them. I learned the hard way about 'friends' being liars. I am so astounded still to remember how they looked so honest and innocent and told me untruths. So be aware that the world is not all what it is saying it is to you. Let your children be aware not to take people seriously and if they have friends, they should be introduced to you, and you should always ask them questions whenever you get a chance. You should know their parents, know what their cell phone numbers are and their addresses. It is your right as a parent to know these things. What is important to you is that your children are protected, as you too, must protect yourself and your spouse.

What is also important to know is, that those who follow Jesus will always be put on the spot. One friend of mine, named Mary, was recounting one Lent that she revealed to her coworkers and boss that she gave up Starbucks for Lent. When she said that she had already broken her pledge to give up that beverage, her boss gave a crow and laughed, saying that his group contributed to the corruption of someone named "Mary". The Blessed Virgin Mary has been a target of calumny from people from the time of her Son's crucifixion, and maybe even before. It is terrible that people of God, followers of Jesus, are targeted throughout history. These times are no different. To be a Jesusian is to be always put into trial like Jesus went through. Everyone knows they have a cross to bear, as did Jesus. But no one seems to understand this is the 'rule' that Satan has put on them.

To wear a crucifix, a medal of the Blessed Virgin Mary, or a Saint, is like wearing a huge sign saying "Persecute Me" to others. One has to be sure to know that Jesus will be with everyone who is not afraid to deny Him.

I don't wish to frighten those who are thinking this and realizing it. But you must be staunch in your faith, keep praying to God, and to Jesus and to ask the Holy Spirit to be your counsel. Ask St. Michael, the Archangel, to guard you at all times. Keep Holy Water close by to sprinkle over you and your surroundings and your home.

Chapter Twenty-One

"You are salt for the earth. But if salt loses its taste, what can make it salty again? It is good for nothing and can only be thrown out to be trampled under people's feet."

Mt 5:13

This passage has been a mystery to me and I am sure it isn't to a lot of Jesusians who have been trained in Biblical truths. But, I have to recount a dialogue I had with somebody I know who told me that she attended Church only on days when she could get off work. She worked in a store and her schedule was not always the same. I felt a bit sad and somewhat put off by what she said. She seemed like the person who, like what Jesus said, had lost their saltiness. It was like she was a lukewarm Jesusian. Neither salty nor dull, just somewhat lacking in that essence that made her authentic, that would have made her a true follower of Jesus.

Granted, not everyone can make it to Sunday Mass. But the Church has given us a lot of choices when, during the weekend, they should make it to Mass. If this woman truly wanted to, she could have made it to Mass and she could have gone every Sunday. God said in the Commandments to honor the Lord's Day. It is sad that people do not persist in their Faith. True followers of Jesus should always persist in their duties to love, honor and follow God. God is always looking for those who are penitent and wish to improve their faith, to improve their saltiness. I think that those who ask Him to help with things like making it to Church every Sunday will find that He will make it possible and He will open up opportunities that they could not see in the first place.

The devil makes it a point to make people of God confused, blind, and deaf to God's words and what God shows them in their lives. To call upon God's name is to drive away the devil. Jesus' name is what makes the devils fly away. Recall in the Gospel how the devil knew that Jesus is God. Because the followers of Jesus are His sheep, they will always have His protection.

Chapter Twenty-Two

"Therefore, anyone who infringes even one of the least of these commandments and teaches others to do the same will be considered the least in the kingdom of Heaven; but the person who keeps them and teaches them will be considered great in the kingdom of Heaven."

Mt 5:19

There was once a clever remark made by some people I knew or read in a book that said the following: "I frequently break the First Commandment." They say this with an offhand way and laugh self-deprecatingly. I used to wonder and think why they would feel so 'proud' to be one to break one of the Ten Commandments. I suppose that a lot of people like to say the Lord's name in vain and it's awful. Once, a religious sister said in class that if anyone says God's name in vain, God actually comes to see what is going on. He personally sees the one who has called His name and then – well, you can surmise what He might say or Do.

I don't like to talk this way as a rule. I admit to saying an oath and I've confessed it. I wonder whether, though, making a joke of it and trying to look "cool" might be more of a serious offence than breaking the Commandment itself? People always try to pass themselves off as a bad Catholic, or as good Catholics once but they no longer are. A couple of people at work were chatting in the cube next to mine, and they said that they both were good Catholic girls but they no longer were; and, yet they were Good Catholics once. This non-sequitur was so irritating to me and I suspect these girls were aiming to make me so.

A lot of times, when I hear someone tell another that they have a "Mega-Catholic" name, like Mary Ann or something like that, it bothers me and makes me wonder why they label people's names like this. It's almost like shaming them for having a beautiful name after the Mother of God. It's like making the names of Jesusian saints *passé* in the eyes of those who might want to christen their children with a good name.

Chapter Twenty-Three

"But I say this to you, if a man looks at a woman lustfully, he has already committed adultery with her in his heart. If your right eye should be your downfall, tear it out and throw it away; for it will do you less harm to lose one part of yourself than to have your whole body thrown into hell."

Mt 5: 29-30

The worst thing a woman can do to herself is to dress in a scandalous way. Hollywood and Vogue magazine and all that sort of meme has made it so desireable to dress in the most salacious and self-destructive way. This passage is something that has drawn some attention in the distant past when one of the former presidents of the United States admitted to lustfully looking at other women. In my mind, a woman can do men a favor by dressing modestly and not inviting them to commit the sin of lust. Some women might draw umbrage at this statement but it is something to consider when there are a host of women these days who brag and tell stories of being made to have sex with presidents, politicians, Hollywood magnates to get paid in terms of money or status or jobs. And, of course, there are also women who cry Rape when they really had consensual sex with the man they accused. Indeed, if women dressed with care and kept their assets hidden, they would be respected and they would not end up trying to fend off a would-be attacker or rapist.

I might be pilloried for this but I think I have to make a point that this world of men and women has to understand that the human body is a great and wonderful Creation of God. Therefore, being of God, these 'humans' must keep their bodies sacred. Our bodies are Temples of the Holy Spirit. A Jesusian minister from China reminded me of this when he saw me in a flimsy summer dress, which made me feel embarrassed. I now think that in terms of dressing more modestly.

I did not dress modestly when I was much younger. In college, I tried to look like the Vogue magazine models, complete with makeup. But, as I went through life, I also went through life with my dear, departed mother, Sally, who would take a look at me first thing out of my room to comment on my dress. There were many days when I had to go back into my room to change my clothes. So, for mothers out there, you have a job to do for your beautiful daughters: teach them to dress modestly. It will save you and her a great deal of suffering and pain.

Chapter Twenty-Four

"Do not store up treasure for yourselves on earth, where moth and woodworm destroy them and thieves can break in and steal. But store up treasures for yourselves in heaven, where neither moth nor woodworm destroys them and thieves cannot break in and steal. For wherever your treasure is, there will your heart be too."

Mt 6:16

It is hard to think of this passage in terms of its effect on me. I really love this passage, not only because it's true but because I am glad I do not have wealth of money or house or brokerage accounts. I think a lot of people, those who are Franciscans, for example, would love to give all of their riches to have heaven. If only the rest of the world would feel this way.

When I was a young girl, in high school where many wealthy girls attended, I was invited to a birthday party. In those days, my family had no car, we were quite poor in the eyes of the world. My mother and I took a cab to the girl's house in the pouring rain. When we got to the house, we were greeted by their servant who looked at the cab wonderingly. "Oh," he said, "you didn't bring your car?" My mother, trying not to betray our poverty, answered, "Oh, we didn't want to ruin our car because of the rain." The servant left it at that and I went in while my Mom went back home in the cab.

These days, it's a given to have a car when a person turns sixteen. A lot of people in the rest of the world, outside of the USA, would give their eye teeth to own a car. Sometimes, I walk past a pedestrian, waiting for the bus with grocery bags or walking to their small apartments with a bag of food and I wonder whether they might need to have a car instead of walking. It's almost rare to find anyone walking in my little city and many of these pedestrians are from another country and cannot afford to buy a car.

I think we all have to find ways to give our wealth away. We must at least give to those who ask us, those who have suffered misfortune, those who may have lost everything in a catastrophic accident. We have to take care of the poor and those who have nobody to take care of them.

Many of those who work have become so successful that they have bought stock or ETFs and watch the market go up and up or come down. Their lives are fraught with fear that their retirement funds will become small when they finally hang up their hats and enter the retiree list. One time when the market was really coming down and people were shaking in their boots about a Crash, my boss decided to put all his stock into money funds. He was of retirement age and he didn't want to lose out on what his money had earned him for decades.

I think that the preoccupation of this world is the market and its swings. I hope that at least people should name a charity a beneficiary of their 401k's and see how they can also invest in small cap funds to help small businesses. Being socially conscious and more Jesusian-like, for example, by buying stock of businesses that are Pro-Life is also a good idea.

I believe that there are also organizations, like the Franciscan Missions, where you can donate jewelry to help them fund their priests who are serving in distant countries, alone most of the time and needing help and medicines. You can also donate old eyeglasses and things that could be used by those less fortunate. Donating to the Native Americans is also a good idea. Children of Native American origins are so under-educated and undernourished in so many ways. Why don't you think of donating a gift card to these groups? Once an acquaintance lost her house in a fire and she and her husband had to stay in a hotel while they got their things in order. Our group of friends donated gift cards from Macy's, or Applebee's, or Panera for them so they didn't have to rely on hand me downs, which I think they also appreciated.

Consider shopping down and not trying to add to a burgeoning closet full of new clothes. Give your old but still good-looking clothes to the poor before buying a new outfit. Give new clothes to orphanages and those who care for pregnant mothers who have been cast out by uncaring families or boyfriends/husbands. One good organization is Good Counsel, based in NY. It is a great and worthy charity and helps to house and educate new Moms and keep safe their children while their Moms go to school or work. This charity is also good in that it helps to keep women from going for abortions. It is important that these women know that there is a good and worthwhile alternative to abortion. We must let them know that Jesusians are prepared to help them with raising their children and not leave them alone after they've given birth.

Chapter Twenty-Five

"Jesus said to him, 'I will come myself and cure him.' The centurion replied, 'Sir, I am not worthy to have you under my roof; just give the word and my servant will be cured.'"

Mt 8:7-8

This passage is one that is familiar to many who come to Mass regularly. We receive Jesus in the Holy Eucharist and say this very sentence – "My God, I am not worthy to receive Thee, but only say the Word and I shall be healed."

How many of us Catholics know that Jesus is Present in the Holy Eucharist? How many believe this fact? Jesus IS in the Holy Eucharist and He dwells in us, in our bodies, for as long as the Host is there. Somewhere I read that Jesus remains in our bodies for 15 minutes after Holy Communion. That is a good length of time to meditate and be on our best behavior. But many of those who receive Him go flying out the door and race their cars out the parking lot of the church right away. And some of us behave badly just after leaving the Church. I am not exempt for I once lost my temper at something right after coming out of the church and then I remembered and felt really sad.

I hope everyone who reads this knows that Jesus' Presence in the Eucharist is what sets the Catholic

Church from other religions and all those denominations that came after Luther left the Catholic Church. A great number of converts should know this and believe this. Easter Sunday should be the happiest time in a newly baptized Jesusian's life. It's not always like this and that is a problem that happens many times after Easter Mass has been said and finished.

One of my former coworkers was a convert and sang in the choir. I didn't see her very often but whenever I did, I talked to her and asked her how things were going. I discovered that she quit the choir (which I did notice) and then she revealed that she stopped going to Mass altogether. It was a surprise to me, but I couldn't ask her why she stopped going. I should have asked, but something stopped me. There are moments like these when one is confronted with a disappointing response that merits comment but possibly merits being given to

God in prayer. Those who wanted so much to be a part of the Catholic church, yet fall away, have to be asked "Why?" Why bother going through RCIA? Why bother with the Rite of Admission, the Baptismal Rite, the Confirmation? Is this only something that people put in their bucket list? Whatever has kept them from returning is probably a work of satan and no one else. Some of these who have gone through RCIA never really come back to Mass any more for the reason that they never really cared and they were possibly coerced by a family member just to get married in the Church. It's a possibility. It's a lot of other reasons. Nobody really can know except God.

What is very crucial is that these people are missing the Grace of Holy Communion, and the Grace of Reconciliation, among others. The Sacraments are so important to the life of a Catholic. The Presence of Jesus in you makes You a holy, healed and happy person. Life without Jesus's Body and Blood is like being out in the cold always. In the cold, rainy, and clammy gutter of life. In the wasteland where dead people reside; dead in their sins, dead to God, headed into Hell forever.

Chapter Twenty-Six

"And when Jesus reached the house the blind men came up to him and he said to them, 'Do you believe I can do this?' They said, 'Lord, we do.' Then he touched their eyes saying, 'According to your faith, let it be done to you.' And their sight returned."

Mt 9:28-29

"According to your faith, let it be done to you." It strikes me here that we receive grace and healing according to the amount of faith we have in Jesus.

Those who remember how nobody in his home town thought much of him should remember that Jesus could do no miracles there. I believe that is so in this life as well. Those who believe implicitly in Jesus' ability to do wonderful things for them in their lives will have what they need and more. Those who feel unable to believe or have faith in Jesus's love for them, His desire to do good things for their salvation will not get to Heaven. The salvation of Jesus's followers is shown in this passage. You, as Catholics, should believe, really BELIEVE, in Jesus's Power and Might to make it to Heaven.

We, as ordinary people, go through life and suffer and get bogged down so much so that we forget that Jesus is the Source of All that is Good. The devil works hard day and night to keep us from lifting up our hearts in prayer. The devil wants us to stop praying, to stop going to Mass, to stop receiving the Sacraments. Because each of these Things will open our eyes to what is really happening in our lives. Jesus is our Savior. He heals. He touches our lives and makes it better. He looks at all of our problems, our family members, and those who work with us in the offices and stores and makes it easier for us to bear all. Most important of all, Jesus heals our minds and hearts so that we will always be IN HIS SACRED HEART.

Chapter Twenty-Seven

"So if anyone declares himself for me in the presence of human beings, I will declare myself for him in the presence of my Father in heaven. But the one who disowns me in the presence of human beings, I will disown in the presence of my Father in heaven."

Mt 10:32

I knew a woman once who, before meals, would not make the Sign of the Cross and say grace in a public restaurant, but instead would pause and think of the prayer before diving into her food. I know that a great deal of pressure is put on Catholics to declare their Faith in public. I try to say grace every time I face my meal, and so do a good number of my Catholic friends. Yet, even those who profess to belong to Marian groups in my church or in other places, forget to say grace and make the Sign of the Cross.

When passing a Church, old-fashioned respect requires that one make the Sign of the Cross. I remember an Irishman talking about it on a Catholic network, and it evoked a great reaction from the audience. Some places have this ingrained in their citizens and yet we do not do this in this country, where we should be so very grateful for the blessings of living in it.

We all must be grateful and acknowledge God, our Savior, and God, our Heavenly Father, and God, the Holy Spirit, for getting us our daily Bread, our homes, family, belongings and jobs. We all must acknowledge Their Presence in our lives. There are so very many who have fallen away from this practice and we cannot allow this to go out of our consciousness.

In an earlier chapter, I spoke about how Social Media has become the purveyor of 'political correctness' in this age and culture. We all must be careful that social media does not remove our Holy Imprint in our psyches and our bodies.

In my experience, speaking out for what's right is the way to 'declare ourselves for Jesus in the presence of human beings'. We cannot turn away from His Teachings. Without Him, where would we all be? He suffered and died for our sins. He went through Calvary for us, so that we might know how to follow Him in our lives. He rose from the dead, and ascended to Heaven so that we, too, can have the confidence that, if we followed Him, we too, can have Heaven.

Chapter Twenty-Eight

"Do not suppose that I have come to bring peace to the earth: it is not peace I have come to bring, but a sword. For I have come to set son against mother, daughter-in-law against mother-in-law; a person's enemies will be the members of his own household."

Mt 10:34-35

When I had a conversion a long time ago while working in a university lab, I became aware of how my deepening love for Jesus was beginning to cause a few people there to start talking about me. I was told that when I wore the

St. Benedict crucifix, that I "looked like a nun." When I was in the elevator with a woman from another department, she looked at my Miraculous Medal with hate. She commented on it and made me feel disappointed that someone could spew such a passionate hatred for the Mother of God. I didn't proselytize there, merely wore what I felt would keep me close to God. Later in my life, when I became more outspoken against abortion, I suffered ostracism in my workplace. I became a target. That was Jesus' effect on my life. Was it worth it? Yes. It separated me from those who hated Him, and He in turn, protected me in ways that I still cannot fathom but I know that He was instrumental in how my life had taken a better turn for good.
I was not the only one in my family who suffered.

I'm not a social person anyway, and now, I find that the society of others is difficult to undergo. I now understand why there are those who prefer their own company than the company of those who lack the same interests and outlook as me. For example, I used to enjoy lunches with coworkers and then I sat with a group in a restaurant where some people voiced their hatred for Chick-Fil-A. This restaurant has received a great deal of criticism and vitriol for their pro-traditional marriage views. I sat there feeling the urge to insist on their right to free speech, yet, I was held mute. Then, this man brought up the subject of nuns wearing wedding rings. This made me speak up and say informatively, that when they are professed, they become Spouses of Jesus. The group sat silent and they changed the subject. Since that moment, I decided that my own company was much preferable to others whose views aren't interesting to me, aren't kind to others, are hateful in their speech and are malicious in their intent. It was a good idea for me to practice solitude in the midst of a world that cared so much about currying friendships and society. I may be the odd woman out, but I decided that the friends I preferred were those who have no qualms about their love and faith for God – the followers of Jesus. These were the people who I consider as saints.

Another event that happened to me when I felt frustrated by the lack of friendships (this was earlier in my life), I decided to go home for lunch and sat by myself in our apartment, surrounded by the statues of Jesus and the Blessed Virgin Mary, the statues of the Holy Saints and their images. In a short while, I decided that I would "pretend" that these Holy Persons were there with me and so I prayed to them to accompany me with my meal. I decided that they would not mind if I gave them my thoughts, and I felt better afterwards. I suppose this might be an extreme case to some, but when Jesus intervened in my life by causing my conversion, I think you can appreciate how it was for me to be removed of the good company of human beings. Resorting to having meals with the Saints was much preferable to me and I still invite Them to dine with me during mealtimes and snacks.

Chapter Twenty-Nine

"Anyone who finds his life will lose it; anyone who loses his life for my sake will find it."

Mt 10:39

This passage has always stumped me. I heard homilies about this from my parish priests and read about it from devotional books. Yet, it puzzled me. Here is Jesus being The Poet Extraordinaire. I could not figure it out and it just haunted my thoughts whenever it came up in the Gospel Readings.

I figured out that it could be this: Those who have a life that they find suitable to the point of being ensconced in comfort and luxury, with friends that had influence, who themselves were influential, and had the funds to retire in good comfort or better – these are the people Jesus means in the first part of the passage. These people will LOSE their comfortable lives.

Those who lose their lives, will find them. It means to me, that those who, because of their allegiance to their Faith, their love for Jesus, their devotion to the Blessed Virgin Mary, will have their lives given to them in ways they have not dreamed of. It is as simple as that. You know that the poetic way Jesus speaks is what is important to note here. You might think: Oh, I have to die (in the natural way of things) and find my life. It isn't only that simple – yes, you can die and go to Heaven, that's something that can happen. But it's more – you can lose your life by different ways: you lose your job because you spoke up for your beliefs; you lose your life because your beloved has a long term illness that means you need to spend time and money to keep that Person comfortable; you lose your life because you suffer scandal to your name and reputation. In these losses, God is testing you to see what you will do. Will you continue to be faithful to Him? Will you turn to Him in your misfortune and ask Him to forgive you for whatever you have done to make Him suffer? Will you stay with your Beloved until that Person has either recovered or died, or will you dump them like some used linen and find another one to take their place?

Once I knew a man who had two ex-wives and a new wife. I met him when he was married to his second wife. They had a rich life. A beautiful mansion. Two cars that were new and flashy. A life of travel and lots of commissions from his wife's job. Then, his wife got sick and she became needful of his attention. He couldn't take it. And then his wife's job fizzled out because she was always absent. The money stopped coming in. So, the man divorced her. He couldn't care less about her then. And then, he took up with a woman who was slim and blonde and had a nice sense of fashion. Arm candy, is what they might be called. There was another man I also met who was full of fun, loved to joke, a regular guy. I learned that his wife had breast cancer. I saw them at a supermarket shopping and met his wife. She wore a turban because her hair had fallen out leaving her bald – the consequences of chemotherapy. They had several children. All grown. Later after a few months, he stopped talking about her. I didn't know what happened. He said to me in a conversation that he couldn't stand being sad, suffering, going through pain. He said that he had to leave this situation because he just couldn't take it. This man spent a lot of time moving out and moving in to different places and jobs. He just couldn't stand going through a hard patch in life. He never saw that this was the test and sadly, he just became the shallow person that he always was – stuck in a very bad relationship and fooling himself that his life was great. He never spoke about his kids. He seemed to be alone more than not, and never gave me the impression that his kids ever talked to him. My thought is, that when he left his sick wife, his kids left him and stayed with her.

Chapter Thirty

> "'Again, the kingdom of Heaven is like a merchant looking for fine pearls; when he finds one of great value he goes and sells everything he owns and buys it.'"
>
> Mt 13:45

In my mind, this is Jesus' Final Statement about what He thinks Heaven is all about. I used to collect jewelry, addicted to the home shopping networks and to shopping in the malls. I no longer wear much jewelry and I am sure that this will go for the rest of my life. I think that my addiction to shopping, to jewelry, was borne out of a desire to feel happy. They call it "retail therapy". I had a life that wasn't great and my profession was out of my reach.

My workplace dealt with the offal of dead animals, roadkill, and disease. It was not the best place for someone like me but that was all I could find because I lost my 'real' job to the call of my boss' new workplace. He left us for a better job (for HIM) in the East coast. Because I didn't want to move to follow him (as some people in research do), I stayed and took what was offered. So, I guess my feelings of worthlessness gave me the urge to fill what was lacking by buying rings and earrings and necklaces and clothes and shoes and everything. This is probably the most extreme that I – as any woman – went through. I had no boyfriends nor did I have friends that I felt could be relied on to stay. It seemed that what friends I made left after a while – for their new jobs out of state or to return to their countries to take up a good place in academia. So, I guess that was why I got into the habit of shopping. It gave me no satisfaction. In fact, I told myself when considering buying yet another gemstone ring, that I only had ten fingers and it wasn't realistic to buy another ring to add to the collection when I only used one finger in each hand to wear a ring! I got the message after a while. That message came from a priest who spoke in a Mass that I happened to attend one weekend. He was someone that I felt directly spoke to me about what I ought to do with all my material things. He persuaded me to give up my 'stuff' and send it to the less fortunate. He was so effective that I actually went home and put my old but good clothes in a bag and gave it to the thrift store. I also looked through my rings and necklaces and put them in a bag to send to the Franciscans. It was a relief.

I did not send all my rings – many of them were my Mom's and Dad's gifts to me. So those were cherished. But, what was important was that I did come to realize that Heaven isn't found in material things nor is it found in retail therapy.

Chapter Thirty-One

"'In truth I tell you, if your faith is the size of a mustard seed you will say to this mountain, 'Move from here to there,' and it will move; nothing will be impossible for you."

Mt 17:20

This passage is Jesus' message for those who have the smallest of faith in their hearts. Remember when the centurion asked Jesus to "Help my unbelief"? This is what we all should pray to Jesus so we can have an increase in faith that He will bring us to Heaven.

Chapter Thirty-Two

"'I must proclaim the good news of the kingdom of God to the other towns too, because that is what I was sent to do.'"

Lk 4:42

Jesus started the missionary ministry in his life, and after He ascended to Heaven, He left that to His Disciples. All twelve of them were scattered to all of the four corners of the Earth to spread the Good News.

Nowadays, it seems that the missions are lacking in vocations to spread Jesus' Good News and they are living in fear of being attacked by terrorists. Some are eager to work but the conditions in which they live are subpar and they have to make it through to the end of their assignments.

What we, as Catholics, must do is to help the Missionaries by sending donations of however any amount. At least a donation for the missionary to say a Mass for one or more of your deceased or living relatives. They need to know, these stalwart priests, that they are NOT alone, that they are supported by those back home and that their work is going to gather more souls to Heaven. And those who send them financial support will also go to Heaven, no matter how much they give and how often they send money. It isn't only money but prayers and sacrifice that are needed to help support the Missionaries.

Churches must be open to the Missionary Priests when they come to visit to ask for donations and prayers. We must each of us find it in our hearts to open them to God's urging to give of our funds to help. This world is not going to survive without the help of those who are still able to and willing to forego a nice meal in a restaurant so they can give the money to support the Missions.

It was sad for me when I learned that our new priest in our parish did not open the church and Masses to those Missionaries who came to visit the diocese. He did, however, support a 'sister parish' in a place in Africa where donations were sent to help put up a decent school to teach the children there.

However, Jesus' words "Give to those who ask." should be ringing in our ears whenever a letter from the missions comes to your mailbox. I know that there are so very many of these charities who ask for help, but you need to be able to discern with prayer to whom you can send financial help.

Those who are sending money in coins with their letters of need are not to be given any more money. It seems that these organizations have enough money in nickels to send to a thousand donors and I find that difficult to respond to. It is not a good idea to send as though one were 'priming the pump' to get more money back. It's a practice that smacks of Wall Street, not the missions.

Those who are sending requests for donations from shrines and from those who are supposedly saints in heaven are going to be in trouble with God because it is only God Who decides who these Saints are. The plethora of sainthood commissions that came within the past fifty years under John Paul II are not fully vetted and there is doubt that even Mother Teresa is really a saint. So, be aware that those who pray to a saint will likely not be answered because that saint is NOT in Heaven.

It is best to pray to Jesus, St. Joseph, St. Michael the Archangel and Our Blessed Virgin Mary, and, always to God to have our intentions heard.

Chapter Thirty-Three

"Be compassionate just as your Father is compassionate. Do not judge, and you will not be judged; do not condemn, and you will not be condemned; forgive, and you will be forgiven. Give, and there will be gifts for you: a full measure, pressed down, shaken together, and overflowing, will be poured into our lap; because the standard you use will be the standard used for you."

Lk 6: 36-38

It seems that the modern world is so busy and full of

people intent on doing what they have on their agendas and cell phones. They walk around with their heads bent to check their messages and text, not even really looking around whether they were stepping into a puddle or bumping somebody on the way.

When I lived in New York, I took the 6 train to Manhattan and got off at the Bloomingdales' exit. There, I saw homeless people lying on the grate, on the gutter, with their cardboard boxes for privacy, and their old ragged coats to cover them from the cold. It bothered me a great deal and yet I didn't have any idea how to help any of them. Everyone stepped over these homeless. At some point, the mayor and the powers that were in those days decided to pack all the homeless and put them into a new building so that they wouldn't be eyesores. But I wonder whether this was an expedient thing they did (it didn't look good for the city's merchants to have a homeless man lying in front of their storefront) or not.

What I'm trying to say is, that one must find it in themselves to be compassionate to those less fortunate, to those who have lost jobs, those who suffered rejection from anyone. It is a harsh life to live in a city like New York, where everyone expects to conquer it by any means necessary. This is a lesson people need to learn and not a lot of them learn it the way God wanted them to. I think People of God should be aware that ignoring the poor is a bad thing and will not earn them a place in Heaven.

I once crossed a crowded street in New York City, and got accosted by a homeless man asking for money. I did not carry a lot of cash but I had a coin purse full of coins and so I gave him most of the contents. We smiled at each other and he left me happily. If only to get someone to react with a smile, one should practice compassion. One must try to be considerate of other's feelings. Rudeness doesn't make you clever or smart, it makes you a candidate for the flames of Hell. You can be considerate and listen with a compassionate heart to anyone who suffers a blow, either at work or in your circle of friends. There, you will find who your friends are.

Friends are very few – true friends to be specific. One can only count on your Holy Angel who guards you to keep you out of trouble. Be sure to pray and exalt your Holy Angel, your Guardian, to God frequently so that He will be elevated and made to be more able to keep you away from harm and bad people. Anyone else who professes to be your friend should be given a vetting. There are many who want to be a friend because they have a hidden agenda. Or, you are counted as one of God's friends.

Those who are fake and fair-weather friends are easy to spot. I once sat in a meeting where I was with a number of associates and my boss. I was put on the spot and my boss erupted into a howl that gave me a feeling of humiliation. The room was quiet and I sat there waiting for someone to come to my defense. Nobody came to get me out of the hot seat. It was my show and so I had to make the most of it. Those who I thought would come to see me afterwards to offer their consolation never did. Only one person, who wasn't even in that meeting, came to ask me an off the cuff question and noticed something wrong. I am grateful that this person was kind enough to listen to what happened to me, and I gather that he left the company once he saw this treatment happen to a person such as me. Nobody wants to work for a company that only cares for their employees when things are good. There must be a conscientious ability in any legitimate company to have proper respect for their employees, not to berate them in the midst of others, and attempt to lower their position by means of abusive language.

Chapter Thirty-Four

"And that is why the Wisdom of God said, 'I will send them prophets and apostles; some they will slaughter and persecute, so that this generation will have to answer for every prophet's blood that has been shed since the foundation of the world, from the blood of Abel to the blood of Zechariah, who perished between the altar and the Temple.' Yes, I tell you, this generation will have to answer for it all."

Lk 11:49-51

All through the history of the Catholic Church, God has sent down many prophets and apostles. All of them were cut down, from those who were the likes of St. Stephen, down to Saint John Paul II. Even those who were sent down who were never anyone in fame have been cut down at an early age, long before they were supposed to go to meet the Father. These unknown martyrs, for martyrs they are, may have been your grandparents, your children, your sisters and your brothers, your uncles and aunts, grandparents. People who were staunch Catholics, who wore their rosaries around their necks or a simple Crucifix. These were the people who voiced their objections to what was going on in the world, who voted against abortion-candidates, who made it clear that they were going to Hell. These are the unsung martyrs, whose unseen suffering are now facing God in Heaven pleading for vengeance against those who managed to kill them in their beds or in their hospital rooms or in the streets in a made-up accident.

Yes, there are those who are minions of satan who roam this world seeking to ensnare the righteous and upright in God's Mind. The very streets of this city are rife with these awful, terrorist minions and this is one reason why I have decided to write this book. It is a warning to those who wish to destroy what is Godly, what is Good and Right that God's Warrior Angels are out EN FORCE to seek and destroy them.

Let this warning be a comfort to those who are willing to show their loyalty and fealty to God, their Almighty Father. Let these good people of God stay on this earth without fear of retribution from those who follow the darkness of Evil. That is all.

www.ingramcontent.com/pod-product-compliance
Lightning Source LLC
Chambersburg PA
CBHW031419290426
44110CB00011B/452